THE
Archive Photographs
SERIES

GREAT YARMOUTH
A SECOND SELECTION
WITH GORLESTON AND CAISTER

The Home and Colonial Stores, 11 Broad Row. This shop, next to Engledow and Gallant the jewellers, traded until the 1960s and eventually became part of Plattens.

THE
Archive Photographs
SERIES

GREAT YARMOUTH
A SECOND SELECTION
WITH GORLESTON AND CAISTER

Compiled by
Colin Tooke

CHALFORD

First published 1996
Copyright © Colin Tooke, 1996

The Chalford Publishing Company
St Mary's Mill, Chalford,
Stroud, Gloucestershire, GL6 8NX

ISBN 0 7524 0643 4

Typesetting and origination by
The Chalford Publishing Company
Printed in Great Britain by
Redwood Books, Trowbridge

Contents

Joseph Haylett outside his tobacconist shop, 9 Tan Lane, Caister in the 1930s.

Introduction

This book, the second in the *Archive Photographs* series of Great Yarmouth, has again drawn on large collections of photographs and postcards to illustrate more aspects of the town's past. As in the previous book the date range is approximately one hundred years, from the 1870s to the 1970s. The seven sections have been arranged to give the reader a brief history of the subjects covered and the scope of the book has been extended to include Southtown and Gorleston and, for the first time in a book of this type, the neighbouring village of Caister. Some of the photographs are before living memory but they all form part of a complex jigsaw that, over the years, has helped to piece together a comprehensive pictorial history of the town and the surrounding area. The majority of the photographs were taken by unknown photographers, some commercial, some amateur, but they combine in this book to form a record of the past for us to look back and reflect upon. The twentieth century photographs will bring back memories for many readers, the extensive damage caused to the town by the Second World War and the terrible aftermath of the 1953 floods, still vivid in the minds of many local people. By extending the area covered south to Gorleston and north to Caister the book will be of interest to those who lived, and still live, in these areas. Both Gorleston and Caister have grown from small nineteenth-century villages to become main residential areas to the adjacent town. The photographs have been drawn from many sources including the collections of John Taylor, Alec McEwen, Barry Temple and the late Edward Goate The photographs of the 1953 floods are the work of a local professional photographer, the late Donald R. Nobbs, used in this book with the permission of his son. To the people named above and many others who have offered me photographs, allowed me to look at their collections and advised on the contents of the book I am most grateful and take this opportunity to thank them all. For assisting me in the final selection of photographs, helping with the layout and being patient and understanding during the time it has taken to compile this book, I would like to thank Jan.

The rear of houses in Gorleston High Street as seen from the river and Darby's Hard. The house on the left is No 1 High Street, for many years the home of Percy Darby, shipbreaker. The houses on the right are in High Road, Southtown.

One

Southtown
and Gorleston

From the beginning of the nineteenth century Southtown became the home of many Yarmouth merchants, handsome houses lining one side of the Southtown Turnpike while timber yards, wharves and ship yards lined the river bank. In 1867 a Yarmouth historian wrote 'at the present day Southtown contains many neat and commodious private residences and forms an agreeable suburb of Yarmouth'. Gorleston, originally a small fishing and farming community on the high ground overlooking the mouth of the river Yare, became part of the Borough of Great Yarmouth in 1832. By the mid-nineteenth century it was still a small settlement and the combined population of Gorleston and Southtown was below 4,000. Towards the end of the century Gorleston began to develop as a holiday resort, designed as a quiet alternative to its neighbouring and sometimes noisy Great Yarmouth and it expanded southwards along the cliffs, away from the old centre around the High Street. In 1937 it was described as 'a resort for the discerning holidaymaker'. Following the Second World War large housing developments, to replace the war damaged Yarmouth Rows, were built to the west of Gorleston, dramatically increasing the population.

At 3 pm on 21 October 1930 HRH The Prince of Wales cuts the ribbon to open the new Haven Bridge watched by the Mayor, Alderman A.H. Beevor and Russell Colman, Lord Lieutenant of Norfolk. Behind are members of the council and representatives of the builders Sir William Arrol & Co Ltd. The ribbon was specially made for the occasion by Grout & Co the local silk factory. A bridge has stood on this site since 1427 linking the town with Southtown and Gorleston.

The new Haven Bridge in 1930 with the temporary bridge erected in 1928 still in place. The new bridge cost £200,000, has a total length of 378 feet and the opening leaves weigh 650 tons. The bridge was the seventh to be built across the river at this point.

Shipley's forge and adjoining buildings shortly before they were demolished in 1927 to make way for the temporary bridge. William Shipley started his veterinary practice on this site in 1884.

Several different forms of transport can be seen at the foot of the bridge in the early 1930s. The tram is at the terminus ready for a trip to Gorleston and the advertising hoardings hide the railway sidings from Southtown Station to the quayside. The East Suffolk tavern (pictured below) is on the left.

Louisa Gray was landlady of the East Suffolk Tavern at No. 6 Southtown Road, when this picture was taken in the 1920s. On the right the Bridge Hotel is advertising Bed & Breakfast for 2/6 (12½p). This later became the Birds Eye Social Club.

The Station Beer Stores on the corner of Wolseley Road and Station Road was renamed the Rising Flame in 1974. The Steward & Patteson public house was named after the nearby Southtown Railway Station, closed in 1970 and demolished in 1977.

The Sefton Arms stood on the north side of Sefton Lane. On the right are the four houses in Willow Place, leading through to St Mary's Lane. The landlord was Ernest Crowe until the house closed in 1940.

Southtown Road, looking north *c.* 1885. On the right is the entrance to the Armoury with the two gun barrels outside. (One of these is now mounted outside the Fishermen's Hospital in the Market Place). The soldiers have probably just marched from the Armoury, some of the buildings of which still survive and are today used as offices.

The 'tin mission' on Southtown Road *c.* 1910. The new church never materialised on the site and the houses 246-249 Southtown Road now stand here. The Trinity Church was sometimes called 'Lady Huntingdon's Chapel' or 'Countess Huntingdon's Connexion'

The Half Way House closed in 1968, shortly after this picture was taken, and was demolished in 1970. In the last century the Guardian Angel stood on the site, rebuilt in 1882 as the Half Way, so called because it was the halfway point for the horse trams from Haven Bridge to Gorleston Feathers Plain. The frontage seen here was added in 1938.

The Gorleston Parish Clerk's house in Church Lane c. 1910. The new church hall was not built on the site and a terrace of houses now stands on this north side of the road.

Brush Quay, August 1901. The horse tram is at the terminus and behind it a queue are waiting
to board a pleasure steamer to Yarmouth. On the left is Pop's Meadow and the William IV
public house. In 1904 a new public house was built on the space seen in front of the one
pictured here and today the Seahaven holiday flats occupy the site of the old house. Pavilion
Road runs between the Meadow and the ornamental gardens.

Henry Clay's Pops were a concert party who, from 1925 until 1934, played in a wooden hall on the meadow seen in the previous photograph. The site today is still known as Pop's Meadow. In this 1933 picture of the Pops the three young ladies are Pat West's Gems and Henry Clay is on the far right of the group.

The Anchor & Hope, seen here in the 1880s, was a favourite 'local' for the Gorleston beachmen and fishermen. Today the Pier Hotel, built in 1897, stands on the site.

A small travelling fair on Bells Marsh in the 1920s. The slide is called the 'Alpine Glassade' and beside that are Mrs Hewett's swing boats. This piece of ground was used during the fishing season for gutting and packing herring and in the background can be seen the rails for drying fishing nets. In the far distance are the lifeboat sheds.

A tram in the High Street *c.* 1908 passing the post office (closed in 1910), the Oddfellows Hall and Salvation Army depot. On the right is Bussey's grocery and drapery store, a well-known family firm who ceased trading in 1967. In 1914 Barclays Bank was built on the vacant site in the foreground and today Hughes TV occupies the site of the old post office.

One of the last horse trams in Gorleston, outside what was later to be the Coliseum cinema. The shows advertised on the front of the tram were performed during the week commencing 3 July 1905. Electric trams replaced the horse trams on 4 July 1905.

A collection of political posters outside the Fisher Institute for the General Election of January 1910. The Institute was demolished shortly after this and the new Coliseum cinema built on the site. The cart belongs to D. Bloomfield, bill poster and tent hirer.

The entrance to the Coliseum cinema which opened on August Bank Holiday 1913. The Maypole Dairy is on the right. Ticket prices when this picture was taken were 6d, 9d and 1/- or in today's prices 2p, 4p and 5p.

A late 1920s view of the cinema foyer. The hanging notice says 'silence is essential for the full enjoyment of talking pictures'. Audiences had become accustomed to talking through the silent films and it was difficult to persuade them to listen to a film sound track.

The Palace in Beach Road was also known as the Scala, Playhouse and Louis Quartorze but it opened 21 July 1913 as Filmland. It was destroyed by bombing 24 August 1940 when one person was killed and three injured.

THE PALACE, GORLESTO

Reeves leather merchants 127 High Street c. 1915. By 1920 the shop had become Plattens, who's Gorleston branch traded here until 1985. Today the shop is Blockbuster Video. On the right is the Feathers Inn.

Philip Hammond's hardware shop on the corner of Lowestoft Road and Church Lane c. 1905. The business moved to 138 High Street and later became Coopers. Until the 1970s the corner seen here was Boots the chemist with Woolworth's next door. By 1974 the corner site had become Gaywoods DIY shop and today is a bookmakers.

Gorleston Private Hotel, Pier Plain *c.* 1910. This building is now part of the Conservative Club but was originally Gorleston House, home of Garwood Palmer, founder of the Yarmouth department store in 1837. The grounds extended to Lowestoft Road but were sold for redevelopment in 1888 when Mr Palmer died.

Gorleston church choir outing 1901. The smiling face in the centre of the group belongs to the Revd Forbes Phillips, vicar of Gorleston 1893 to 1917, a leading figure both in the religious and social life of the community, organising such events as the Gorleston Pageant.

Church Road school in 1902. The school opened in June 1884 and closed in 1969. The buildings were used for several years as an annex to the College of Further Education before being demolished in 1994. A row of twenty-one houses is now built on the site, on the corner of Church Road and Fredrick Road.

Nature study class at Church Road school in 1902. Benjamin Peart, the headmaster of the boy's school from 1884 until 1906, is seated at his desk. From 1906 Mr Peart became the Organiser of Education for the Borough and Mr Joseph Thompson took over as headmaster until 1930. In 1932 the school became the Church Road Junior Mixed school.

Two

Along the River

The river has always been the lifeline of the town, a haven for the fishing industry upon which the town once depended and now for the gas and oil industry. The rivers Yare, Bure and Waveney flow through Norfolk and Suffolk into Breydon Water and the Yare continues to the sea, at a harbour mouth constructed in the sixteenth century. The first bridge across the river, replacing an earlier ferry, was constructed in 1427 to link the town with the west bank and Southtown and Gorleston. The North River or Bure was crossed by a bridge in the nineteenth century to join the town with a new road across the marshland to Acle. Along the banks of the rivers industry flourished, ship-yards built timber vessels and wharves and warehouses were constructed for the many types of goods imported to and exported from the town. Fishing boats, drifters, trawlers and shrimpers all had their respective quaysides. The river was also extensively used by holidaymakers, sea trips for the more hardy to the Scroby sands, cruises along the Norfolk Broads and rivers or a leisurely ferry trip from Yarmouth to Gorleston. The following pictures illustrate a few of the activities and scenes along the river in years gone by.

Breydon Water where the rivers Waveney, Yare and Bure meet before the Yare continues through the town to the sea. The railway bridge across Breydon opened in 1903 and closed in 1953. The bridge was demolished in 1962 and today the western by-pass follows almost the same route across this large stretch of open water.

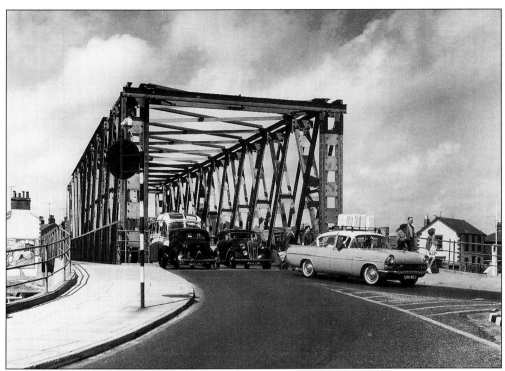

The Callender-Hamilton girder bridge over the river Bure was opened in 1952 and replaced the old suspension bridge built in 1847. Although only intended to last ten years this bridge remained until the present Bure bridge opened in March 1972.

The exit from the above bridge, looking north, in May 1971 with the road passing the river side of the North West Tower and the White Swan. The road was re-aligned the following year with the completion of the new bridge.

The new bridge and road layout looking east in April 1972. The old girder bridge has not yet been removed and beyond that the remains of Laughing Image corner and Rainbow Square where the post office sorting office and Telephone Exchange now stand. There were still extensive sidings at Vauxhall Station at this time, now the Asda site. The brewery buildings had not been demolished and in the distance the Methodist Temple, now the route of Temple Road, can be seen.

Broads excursions leaving Stonecutters Quay in the 1960s. In the distance the *Golden Galleon* makes her way up river while the *Queen of the Broads* and the *Resolute* prepare to leave. In 1968 the *Resolute* was sold to the Veteran Steamship Society. Havenbridge House now stands on the site of the Steward & Patteson building.

The *Yarmouth Belle* at Stonecutters Quay in the late 1930s. This boat made trips to Reedham, St Olave's and Bramerton Woods End during the summer months.

The pleasure steamer *Lily* approaching Hall Quay about 1900. This was the first pleasure boat to run between Yarmouth and Gorleston, the service starting in August 1894. The fare was 2d and the boat carried fifty people. The last sailing of the *Lily* was in July 1903.

The booking office on Hall Quay in the 1920s. From here the Yarmouth & Gorleston Steamboat Co. ran a regular steamer service to Gorleston until 1962 with boats including the *Cobholm*, *Southtown* and *Yarmouth*. Boats also ran to Norwich (2/- return) and Stokesby Ferry (1/-).

Rivers & Broads of Norfolk

Yarmouth & Gorleston Steamboat Co., Ltd.

Daily Trips to Norwich

"YARMOUTH BELLE"
"PRIDE OF THE YARE"
"QUEEN OF THE BROADS"
"WATERFLY"

LIST of REFRESHMENTS.

LUNCHEONS.		WINES & SPIRITS.	
Sandwiches ...	4d.	Port (glass) ...	4d.
Bread & Cheese ...	3d.	Sherry ,, ...	4d.
Beef Patties ...	2d.	Claret ,, ...	3d.
Sausage Rolls ...	2d.	Special Brandy (glass	6d.
Pastry.		Brandy .. ,,	4d.
Oxo (per Cup)	3d.	Irish (Dunville) ,,	4d.
Tea and Coffee (Cup)	2d.	Scotch (Red Seal) ,,	4d,
(Ready at any time)		Gin	4d.
Milk (glass)	1½d.	Rum	4d.
Fruit in Season.		Bottled Ale or Stout	6d.
Gaymer's Cider (bot.)	6d.	Small ditto	3d.
Mineral Waters ,,	4d.	Bass Small	4d.
,, ,, Part	2d.	Guinness Stout ...	4d.
Brewed Ginger Beer	3d.	Cigars	4d.
Glass ,, ,,	2d.	Cigarettes	1d.
Ginger Ale	2d.	,, Packet ...	3d.
Dry Ginger Ale ...	3d.	[OVER	

A list of refreshments available on the pleasure steamers in 1907.

All aboard for a river trip earlier this century.

The paddle steamer *Halcyon* taking on passengers at Hall Quay in the 1890s. The General Steam Navigation Co. ran regular sailing's between the town and London during the summer season. The famous 'Belle' steamers later replaced the GSN services along the East Coast until 1930.

Accidents can happen in a fast flowing tidal river. Here two Navy submarines are trapped against the Haven bridge on Sunday 18 May 1908, caught by the tide while attempting to moor at Hall Quay. A large crowd has gathered to watch the embarrassed Navy who can do nothing until the tide changes.

The *Eastern Princess* in August 1964 making her way down river for a sea trip to Scroby sands.

A timber ship unloading on the west bank of the river in the early 1900s with a wherry moored alongside. The pleasure steamer *Southtown* is coming down river passing a variety of vessels including the fishing smack YH630 moored at South Quay. The *Southtown* left the port for the breakers yard in 1965.

Unloading timber on the west bank in the 1930s. Timber was one of the main imports during the first half of the century, a trade that has today almost disappeared.

Shipbuilding was once an important industry along the river, mainly on the west bank. The Finnish barquentine *Sigyn*, built in 1887, is seen here in Fellows Dock 5 September 1933. This was the last shipbuilding yard on the river, later being taken over by Richards.

The *Antiquity* nearing completion in Fellows shipyard in 1935.

Outside the Gorleston lifeboat shed is the twin funnel steam lifeboat *James Stevens No.3* stationed here from 1903 until 1908. During this time the lifeboat was launched thirty-seven times and saved thirty lives. Only six steam lifeboats were built for the RNLI.

The Gorleston landing stage at Brush Quay in the 1930s. One of the steam pleasure ferries can be seen on the right ready for a trip back to Yarmouth. These double ended boats did not have to turn round in the busy river.

The *Queen of the Channel* began day trips to Ostend in July 1937 and is seen here leaving the quayside in the summer of 1938. As can be seen the trips were very popular. The ship was later sunk in the Dunkirk evacuation.

The *Norwich Belle* entering harbour in August 1970. Built in 1924 at Fellows Dock the *Belle* was converted from steam to diesel in 1958 and finally left the port in 1981 to become a floating restaurant on the Thames. The *Norwich Belle* ran sea trips from Hall Quay during the summer months.

The 'cosies' on the old South Pier at Gorleston were a popular spot for both locals and holidaymakers to fish from or just soak up the sun. On the end of the pier is the coastguard lookout and lighthouse taken down in 1962 before the pier was rebuilt.

Rebuilding the old South Pier started in March 1962 and was completed in February 1964. This picture was taken in August 1962 after a gale had smashed down part of the new piling.

Three

Shops

The advent of the supermarket and out of town shopping has spelt disaster for many small shopkeepers and in particular the traditional corner shops. Many of these small shops have now closed and some are converted into private residences. Long established family businesses have been swallowed up by large conglomerates and familiar names have disappeared. In this section the photographs have been chosen to show a variety of retail outlets, from the corner shop to the large department store and shops selling a wide variety of merchandise. As would be expected in a seaside town there have always been many restaurants and eating houses close to the holiday areas and many of the photographs show the prices of meals offered earlier this century. From hardware shops to newsagents a network of small specialised shops served the needs of the community. In the early 1970s much property in the town centre was demolished to build a shopping precinct and today many of the traditional shopping areas such as King Street and Market and Broad Row have suffered a decline in trade.

The local corner shop was the backbone of the retail trade before the age of the supermarket. For over fifty years the Bradshaw family grocery shop and bakery was on the corner of Salisbury Road and Garfield Road. It is still a food shop today.

Another corner shop in the Newtown area was that of John Whiting seen here in 1922. This was also the North Denes post office, on the corner of Beaconsfield Road and Churchill Road, today a betting shop.

Cotton's Alderson Dairy, seen here in the 1930s with a variety of milk delivery vehicles, on the corner of Alderson and Ormond Roads. Cottons Dairy was founded in 1915 and merged with Collet's Dairy in 1969.

Eager shoppers await the opening of the Northgate Street branch of the Co-op on 30 June 1921. The branch closed in the 1980s and is now the Co-op funeral department.

This unusual building was originally the toll booth on the east side of the suspension bridge on North Quay. After tolls were abolished in 1920 the building, known as the Round House, was used as a boot and shoe repair shop for many years. It is seen here in 1951 just before it was demolished.

Charles Rolling was the original baker at this Northgate Street shop, seen here in 1917 after George Bales had taken over. Row 4 is on the right. Today this is still a bakers shop and the facia and shop front are almost unchanged.

The tobacconist shop of E.W. Goate, 48 North Quay in 1920. Row 34½ is to the left of the shop. In the doorway are Mr and Mrs Goate and their son Edward who was in later life to become one of the town's leading historians and collected of many of the pictures in this book.

Haylett & Son's garage, 175 Northgate Street, in the 1950s. Before the large petrol companies took over the filling stations, garages were able to sell a variety of brands of petrol as seen here.

Until a recent move to new premises in Nelson Road the old established undertaking firm of Brundish & Son occupied these buildings on the corner of Albion Road and Saxon Road.

The southern end of George Street in 1923. Sidney Powell's Dining Rooms are now an antique shop and Buntings the grocers on the right later became Dunbar's (see below). In the distance can be seen the entrance to Broad Row with Middletons newsagents on the corner.

The electrical shop of Dunbar, 9 Hall Quay, in the 1930s. The property between Row 50 and Row 52, including this shop, was demolished in 1970 when Stonecutters Way was constructed from the Quay to Howard Street.

This grand new store for Arnold Brothers opened on the corner of Regent Street 19 May 1906. In 1910 the premises were extended down Regent Street and the old furniture department in Market Row closed. The store seen here was almost totally destroyed by fire 3 February 1919.

An advertising postcard of 1922 for the new Arnolds store. In 1936 the store was sold to the Debenhams chain but retained the old family name until 1972. In 1985 it closed and was partly demolished.

This 1920s advertising card shows Arthurs' Ltd, 18 Market Place. Row 32, Kings Head Row, is to the right of the shop. By the 1960s this was Elmo Food Fare the town's first supermarket.

Smith's Store *c.* 1910 in South Market Road. The shop later became Fields cycle shop and was then converted to a private house. Today the facia and much of the old shop front is still visible.

This shop was at 103 South Market Road in the 1930s. It later became part of Coopers fireplace showroom on the corner of Fish Street and was demolished when the Market Gates shopping complex was built.

Samuel Dodson, pork butcher, outside his shop at 73 Howard Street South in the 1920s. This is a typical example of the small, bow-fronted shops in Howard Street and George Street of this period.

The Toy House, 31 Regent Road *c.* 1928. Standing in the doorway is the owner Mr H. Davis who also owned the shop next door. (see below). Today this is Princes Restaurant.

The Chocolate Shop of Mr Davies, 32 Regent Road, selling Great Yarmouth Velvetbrown Chocolates, *c.* 1928. Today this is part of Vogue.

Regent Road before the first world war when 1/- (5p) dinners and 6d (2½p) teas were available. Beyond the restaurant is Pownalls fishing tackle shop, still trading today. Will the finished sign read FISH DINNERS? Today the restaurant is the Arches and the tea rooms are a clothes shop.

Mr W. Eastoe, newsagent, 172 Middlegate Street in the 1920s. On the left is Row 92 and the north wall of the Unitarian Church, destroyed in wartime bombing.

The butchers shop of Harry Chittleburgh, 72 St Peter's Road, decorated for the 1923 carnival. This shop, on the corner of Nelson Road is today a 'take-away' but the name of Chittleburgh survives in the mosaic doorway.

Middleton's newsagents shop, 73 Victoria Road, 4 September 1899. In the doorway is Mr E. Middleton who was later mayor of the town. Today this is a private house.

King Street *c*. 1922. On the left is Hayden's the opticians and next door at 167 is Woolsey's Stores, jewellers. On the other side of the road is Halford's cycle shop, the Ministry of Labour Employment Exchange, Row 81, Sullivans confectioners and Fieldings cycle shop.

Any article 6½d (3p) was the claim of the Domestic Bazaar at 2 King Street *c.* 1910. This site is now the southern corner of Burton's, Row 64 is on the right.

A winter scene in King Street. The cab is waiting outside Aldred's which in 1926 was demolished to make way for the Central Arcade. Much of the property further along the street was destroyed by wartime bombing.

The restaurant of Reg Ellis on the corner of St Peter's Road and Wellington Road in the late 1930s. This site is now part of the bus station.

Number 28 South Denes Road is today part of Ship Chandlers Ltd. Early this century it was supplying ships with goods under the name of H.J. Hatch. A busy port would have had many small ship chandlers such as this. Cutch was a local name for catechu, a preservative for nets and sails.

Four

Buildings
and Streets

From the beginning of the nineteenth century the town expanded rapidly as new roads were constructed across what was until then open Denes towards the sea. It was the first time in 800 years that the town had been allowed to develop outside the confines of the medieval town wall. Old trackways, leading from the town gates and crossing the barren sand dunes, became new roads eventually to be named St Nicholas Road, Market Road, Regent Road and St Peter's Road, among others. The longest road in the town, Nelson Road, was built to run parallel with the sea and bisect the old tracks. Since the last war new roads have appeared within the old town such as Yarmouth Way, Nottingham Way and Stonecutters Way while the original medieval streets, Howard Street, George Street and Middlegate have been widened or re-aligned. With the new roads came new buildings, many of which survive today. In this section the photographs cover a variety of buildings from the small town cottage to the large residences of the gentry, religious buildings, public houses, buildings of everyday importance and the street scenes that went with them.

These small cottages were in Alfred Place in 1906. A narrow entrance between 19 and 21 Caister Road leads to a small area of lock-up garages which was Alfred Place. In the background is the chimney of the refuse destructor in Tar Works Road.

Number 6 North Quay c. 1906. This was at one time the Lord Collingwood public house, John Bessey being the landlord from 1830 until 1870. The building stood between Row 1 and Laughing Image Corner, now the site of the Telephone Exchange.

This was one of the twenty-five houses in Laughing Image Corner and the one which gave the area its name. It was demolished in 1912 and the two images placed in the Tolhouse museum where they were destroyed by bombing in 1941.

Two old properties in Rainbow Square which led off North Quay. One has the date 1679 on the gable end. The area of Rainbow Square is now covered by the post office.

The Fullers Hill junction with North Quay in 1953. Most of the buildings seen here have now disappeared, the exception being the large Brewery Stores, behind which can be seen the brewery complex of Lacons. In the centre is the church and school of St Andrews. Blocks of flats have taken the place of the houses in the background in Howard Street. A detail of the property on the left is shown on the next page.

North Quay in the late 1930s. Next to the Grocer's Supplies is the North Tower public house, Delf & Son grocers, Row 8, William Smith fishmonger, Brett's furniture repository and three private houses before Fullers Hill. The post office now stands on the site up to Row 8 and the remainder is a car park.

The nave and south chancel of St Andrew's church. This church was built in 1859 and demolished in 1964. A garage for Norfolk Motor Services was built on the site which is now the Comet warehouse, on the corner of Fullers Hill.

Twenty-one delivery vehicles line up outside Lacon's Brewery in the 1950s. The large brewery complex was demolished in 1973 and a new Tesco supermarket and flats built on the Church Plain site.

E. LACON & Co.
LIMITED.
BREWERS,
GREAT YARMOUTH.
(ESTABLISHED 1621.

Spirits of the best quality
VINTAGE & OTHER WINES.

Bottled Beers & Mineral Waters

STORES:
LONDON, CAMBRIDGE, DISS, NORWICH,
LOWESTOFT AND HALESWORTH,

Have also lately acquired the old-established Wine and
Spirit business, known as
BURROUGHS',
1 & 2, Market Place, Gt. Yarmouth.

A Lacons advertisement of 1900. Burroughs' 1 and 2 Market Place is now the Gallon Pot.

A Lacon's delivery vehicle outside the Brewery in the 1960s.

A four-horse brake ready to take an outing from the Royal George on North Quay – destination unknown. The public house was on the corner of Row 37 and closed in the 1960s.

The Conge Mission was at 94 George Street, seen here after adjacent property had been demolished in the 1950s.

This small part of Middlegate survived the war but was soon demolished to make way for new flats. Goulder's, 51 Middlegate, seen here in 1947 was a bakery before the war but re-opened for a short time as a cycle shop.

Some of the large houses at the southern end of Middlegate Street in the 1930s. Looking from Friars Lane the entrance to Row 145, the last row, can be seen in the centre of the picture.

The Tolhouse, Middlegate Street, before its restoration in 1883. The building had housed the local police force from 1836. After it was restored the Tolhouse became the town museum and library until badly damaged in 1941.

The Garibaldi Hotel and annexe in the 1930s. The annexe was originally a terrace of houses known as Northumberland Place leading eastwards to Nelson Road. Note the telephone box to the right.

This postcard, dated 1910, shows the dining room in the Garibaldi which was a 'gentlemen only' hotel.

Since 1955 this building has been the House of Wax in Regent Road but is seen here late in the last century when it was the home of Dr Mitchel. There were many large private houses in Regent Road before the holiday industry took them over.

Regent Road in 1904. The Domestic Bazaar is advertising any article for 6½d. The building to the right became Docwra's Rock factory and further along, Wickens pram shop.

The Catholic church in Regent Road was built in 1850. The large house on the corner with Nelson Road was known as Albert House, seen here *c.* 1880. The corner site became the Savoy Restaurant.

Britannia Terrace, seen here in 1929 before it was commercialised, was originally one of the finest terraces in the town and was built in 1848. Although by the 1920s most of the houses in the terrace had become boarding houses they still retained their original appearance.

The Marlborough Boarding House, 62 Marine Parade, was an example of an unspoilt house in the terrace. Note the private lamp post at the gate.

The Town House or Dutch Chapel, 23 South Quay, was at one time used as a theatre, library and concert hall. The house to the left was replaced by the Port and Haven Commissioners office and the Town House demolished in 1946 after suffering bomb damage during the war. This site is now the roadway to the Central Library.

The Mariners Chapel on the corner of South Quay and Mariners Road was destroyed in the last war. It is seen here in 1870.

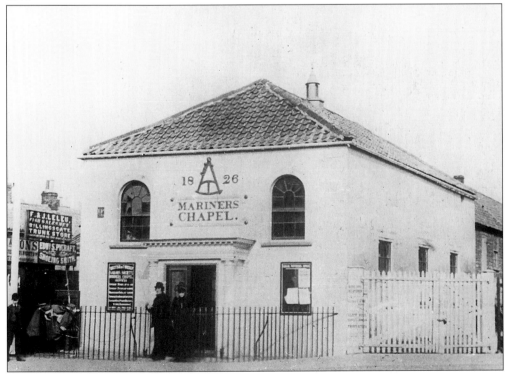

Built by Robert Drury in the seventeenth century this imposing house on South Quay, known as Drury House, was demolished in October 1969 after standing here for nearly 350 years. Next door is the shop of Timothy Blanchflower, a chemist and druggist in 1874.

William Redgrave, grocer, outside his shop at 12 Blackfriars Road in 1906.

Some of the small cottages in Blackfriars Road, built against the town wall and adjacent to the South East Tower in the 1930s.

Blackfriars Road and the SE Tower in the 1870s. On the right is the Victoria Gardens public house.

73

These unusual wooden houses, eight in all, were in Arbon Square, Garden Lane. The lane ran between Friars Lane and Charles Street.

Houses in Friars Lane. The path up the slope behind the railings led to Adam and Eve Gardens and through to Charles Street.

The Gardeners Arms was in Boreham Road which ran parallel to Havelock Road and was demolished in the 1970s re-development of the area. Here a group of locals pose with the landlord John Mann in the early 1920s.

On the corner of Charles Street and Garden Lane was the Garden Lane Tavern, a small beer house which closed in 1939. The Fire Station now stands on the site of Garden Lane.

The Lady Haven public house, Mill Road. Joseph Collins was landlord in 1912. To the left is Collins haircutting shop and on the right is the 'tin mission' of the Congregationalists. The public house was rebuilt in 1956 after suffering war damage.

Five

War and Flood

Two major catastrophes to befall the town this century were the man-made destruction of the Second World War and the natural disaster of the 1953 East Coast Floods, both of which are featured in this section. The war years saw 20,000 properties destroyed or damaged and 217 people killed. Over ninety air-raids brought havoc to both residential and industrial areas of the town as the photographs in this section show. On the night of 31 January 1953 the second disaster of the century arrived in the form of a hurricane force storm and surge tide. An hour before the predicted high tide the river level had risen to overflowing and the sea, whipped up by the hurricane force winds, was already over the sea wall. Later that evening the Breydon river wall was breached and a deluge of flood water descended on the Cobholm area. Nine people died and thousands were evacuated to local holiday camps where many remained for several weeks. The photographs of the floods in this section were taken on Sunday 1 February 1953 and illustrate some of the problems the town had to cope with. They were taken by local photographer Donald Nobbs.

Hills Marine View on the corner of Euston Road and North Drive following an air-raid at 2.30 pm on 31 October 1940.

Four high explosive bombs were dropped on Harbord Crescent at 11.30 am on 10 September 1940. The occupants of this house, No. 40, were killed and five other people injured.

Grout & Co Silk Mill, St Nicholas Road, 1 February 1941. A high explosive bomb dropped on the South Mill causing extensive damage. Throughout the war the factory produced large quantities of parachute silk.

The remains of Reynold's Garage on the corner of Apsley and Rodney Roads after the bombing of 27 February 1941. This raid, the fourth of the day, happened at 2.13 pm when thirteen high explosive bombs were dropped in a line from Apsley Road to King Street. Two people were killed and eighteen injured in the raid.

A parachute mine, dropped at 5 am on 8 April 1941, destroyed the Seagull Garage at the junction of Blackfriars and Queens Road. The garage was also being used as a Special Constabulary Station and five Special Constables were killed. Soldiers, civilians and ARP teams comb the wreckage for survivors.

The aftermath of an early morning raid when five 'planes dropped eight high explosive bombs on the Cobholm area, resulting in twelve dead and thirteen injured'. These houses were in Mission Road.

This high explosive bomb was dropped in Admiralty Road at 3.44 am on 5 June 1941 and failed to explode.

Lacon's Barrel Store, North Quay, after 1,500 incendiary bombs were dropped across the centre of the town on 25 June 1942. The parish church was gutted in this air-raid. The store seen here was rebuilt in 1945 and today is used by Whitbreads as their local depot.

Of the three bombs dropped on 12 June 1941 in Gorleston this one, in Fredrick Road, failed to explode but the others, in Duke Road and Lowestoft Road, killed four people and injured another. The bomb disposal team pose for a photograph after making the 4,000 lb device safe.

A post-war view of the corner of Church Plain. Burrough's Wine Stores had occupied this site until 7 May 1943 when it was destroyed by a direct hit during the first raid by FW190 fighter bombers. In 1959 the Gallon Pot was built on this corner site.

The Wrestlers public house, Church Plain, undergoing repairs following demolition of the adjacent property damaged in the same raid as that on Burrough's Wine Stores.

Tarpaulins cover the damaged roofs of houses in Seymore Avenue following an air-raid on 11 May 1943 when a 500 kilo high explosive bomb demolished the houses that had stood in the foreground. In this breakfast time raid eighteen enemy 'planes made a low level attack, indiscriminately bombing residential areas at the north end of the town.'

Two walkers and a disinterested dog survey the damage the storm and high tides had caused to the Jetty on the night of 31 January 1953.

The Jetty shelters were damaged by the wind and water and later demolished.

On Hall Quay the river had risen to road level and was still high the following morning, 1 February 1953. The wooden blocks which made up the road surface can be seen littering the quayside. The flood walls along the river were built following the 1953 floods.

The low lying section of Southtown Road near the foot of the bridge (sometimes referred to as Bridge Road) flooded. In the background is Southtown Railway station.

A line of vehicles make their way slowly through the floodwater on Southtown Road passing the Two Bears and the Railway Tavern (now The Rocket). The postman on his bicycle carries on with his round the best he can.

A lorry carrying relief workers is followed by a Radio Relays van. The central control room for Radio Relays was on Hall Quay and from there a radio service was relayed by overhead wires to houses in the town.

High Mill Road 1 February 1953. An army lorry approaches a flooded area where even the ducks have to be carried to safety. The Southtown and Cobholm areas were flooded to a depth of several feet by water from Breydon, where the river bank collapsed late in the evening.

Every available boat was used to rescue marooned householders. This canoe, in High Mill Road the morning after the storm, ferries a lady to dry land and safety.

The only way for the workers to get in or out of the maltings in High Mill Road was by boat and ladder. Small boats from the seafront boating lakes and waterways were used in many areas of the town.

A group of residents in High Mill Road salvage livestock (including the cat) and other goods from their flooded houses. It took many weeks for some of the houses to dry out and become habitable again.

A lone policeman rows along Blackfriars Road. In the background is the old Blackfriars post office and Tudman's shop.

Householders are rescued from 56 Blackfriars Road after being marooned by the flood water. The road between the house and the shop is Louise Road.

Six

Leisure Time

Leisure time covers a wide range of subjects and the photographs in this section show but a few of the many leisure pursuits that have taken place in the town, from beach activities of the summer visitor to the theatres and cinemas that provided entertainment throughout the year. From the turn of the century the pace of life has increased and the leisure time that went with it has changed. Victorian and Edwardian visitors were content to stroll along the promenade, sit on the beach, go for a walk in the gardens or take a peaceful ride in a horse brake. As the years went by the types of entertainment changed and amusements, a pleasure beach, mechanical rides and live shows took the place of more sedate pleasures. It is not possible to illustrate here all the entertainment to be found in a sea-side town but pictures have been chosen to give representative examples through the years; the minstrel ring of the late nineteenth century, the travelling circus and fair, the 50s summer spectaculars and the cinema.

Horse racing has been a popular sport in the town for many years. This is the paddock of the old racecourse on the South Denes early this century. The last meeting was held on this course in September 1919 and the new course at the north end of town opened the following year on 15 August.

The world famous circus of Barnum & Bailey visited the town on 28 July 1899. Here the circus parades along South Quay before the performance on the Southtown marshes.

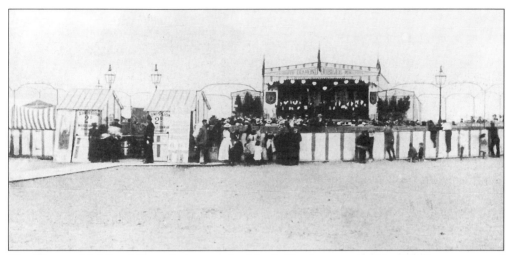

The Diamond Jubilee Minstrel ring on the North Beach, opposite Norfolk Square, opened 5 July 1897. Admission was 2d and there was a seating capacity of 2,000. Performances were given at 11 am, 3 pm and 7 pm each weekday. The last season for these performers was 1909.

WELLINGTON PIER PAVILION.

" THE FOLLIES," had the honour of appearing before their Majesties the King and Queen, at Sandringham, on December 1st, 1905, on the occasion of the Queen's Birthday. MONDAY, September 17th, for SIX NIGHTS, at EIGHT O'CLOCK.

'The Follies', a typical seaside end-of-the-pier show. This group performed at the Wellington Pier in the week commencing 17 September 1906.

Yarmouth fair *c.* 1915. In side-shows such as this the first moving pictures were seen.

A roundabout at the fair *c.* 1910. The children are standing in front of an ice-cream barrow and in the background is a boxing booth.

The Pleasure Beach opened in 1909. The Royal Mountain Scenic Railway seen here opened 20 July 1912 and was destroyed by fire 8 April 1919.

The Circus Zoo was converted to shops in 1973. Before 1935 the Anchor & Hope public house stood on this site and Billy Russell's Dodg'em Track occupied the site before the zoo opened in the 1960s.

Marine Parade, Great Yarmouth

Marine Parade the first week in September 1910. The sandwich-board man is advertising trips to Somerleyton for 1/- and outside Goode's Hotel is a poster for the Vagabonds Concert Party at the Wellington Pier. The 'free exhibition' next to the hotel was later to become the Paradium amusements.

THE PARADIUM.

SOUVENIR OF

GREAT YARMOUTH.

THE WORLD'S SMALLEST MARRIED COUPLE.

This postcard for the Paradium is typical of the 'freak' shows which were popular at fairgrounds and seaside amusements early this century.

This beach scene south of the Britannia Pier dates from the 1890s. Seats are provided at the waters edge while behind are a row of six bathing machines. Next to the 'Skylark Tea Saloon' stalls is a beach photographer while closer to the pier are other refreshment stalls. A collection of sailing boats and steamers provides entertainment for the seated spectators.

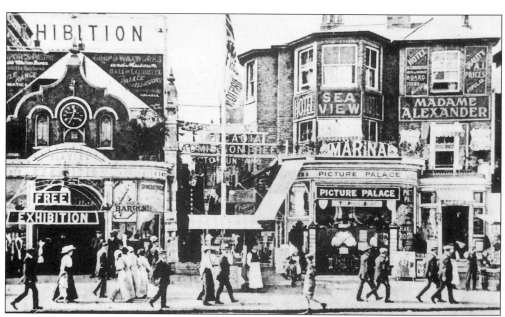

This shows the Marina Picture Palace of the Barron family, the first people to show moving pictures in the town. Mr George Barron played the piano accompaniment. Established in 1896 the Paradium was the forerunner of today's amusement arcades. It is seen here in around 1910.

Tea and ice-cream stalls on the south side of the Britannia Pier in 1909. The splendid pavilion on the pier was destroyed by fire in December the same year.

An eager group of children waiting for their cornets and wafers at a beach stall c. 1910.

Donkey rides have always been a popular sea-side attraction. With the donkeys are goat carts which took children for rides along the prom until 1911.

A predecessor of televised cricket, the Johnnie Walker score board in the Wellington Gardens in 1934. Information from the test match ground was relayed by telephone and the score continually updated on the board. In the centre a magnetic board showed the position of the ball after each stroke.

The open air Marina theatre was opened in 1937 and could seat 4,000 people. It was still popular in the 1950s as the queues here show. The Marina Leisure Centre now stands on this site.

Neville Bishop first played at the Marina in 1938. He is seen here with his orchestra, the Wolves, during the 1953 season.

The Empire opened as a cinema in
1911. The film advertised here was
shown in the week commencing
25 July 1936.

The Regent theatre opened on Boxing Day
1914. On 19 August 1929 it was the venue for
the first talking picture to be shown in the
town.

Advertising a Harold Lloyd film at the Fish Wharf in the 1930s. Driving the car is Mr E.
Bowles, manager of the Empire. Note the horn-rimmed glasses and tiny straw hats issued to the
fisherfolk as advertising material.

Both the Empire and the Gem were showing this new Chaplin film for the week commencing 3 September 1928.

This is Your Laugh ran for the 1958 summer season from 10 June until 20 September at the Windmill Theatre. Parked outside the theatre is the Jaguar car belonging to Jack Jay the proprietor.

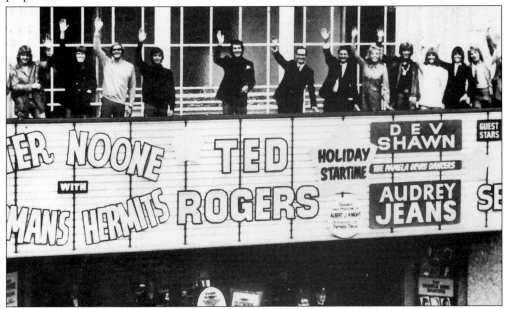

The summer show line-up at the ABC Theatre in 1970. On the balcony, to the left of Ted Rogers, is the theatre manager of many years, Jack Hare.

The Theatre Royal in Theatre Plain closed 12 January 1929 and the last show was the pantomime, *Aladdin*. The theatre stood derelict until demolished to make way for the new Regal theatre which opened in 1934.

Air trips over the town were available in 1922. This 'plane operated from the South Denes and a trip cost 5/- (25p). In the 1950s and 60s air trips were available from the North Denes airfield for 10/6 (52p).

Left: The stage of the Theatre Royal in 1902 when the programme included a mixture of comedy, drama, farce and minstrel shows. The local paper announced 'the management will do all in their power to render the theatre cool and all members of the audience will be sprayed with Sweet Lavender as they enter'.

Bellamys the butchers of 136 King Street with their float which won 3rd prize in the 1924 Yarmouth Carnival. On the left, in the apron, is Claud John Green, manager of the King Street shop.

The Caister Camp entry for the 1924 Yarmouth Carnival.

Seven

Caister

The present day village of Caister, with a population approaching 10,000, is a very different place from that in the first half of this century. What was once a small fishing and farming community has grown into a dormitory for nearby Great Yarmouth, the shops and trades traditionally associated with a self-contained village have disappeared. The photographs in this section show something of what the village was like in the first half of this century, the shops, trades, street scenes and people who lived, worked and came for holidays in the village. Although connected to the nearby town by train and tram the village was able to retain its separate identity for many years. The lifeboat has always played an important role in the life of the village and the holiday industry developed from the early years of the century. A 1928 guide book described Caister as 'not an assertive place… the small voice of Caister-on-Sea is not infrequently unheard by those holidaymakers who search each year for an idyllic little seaside place wherein they can find infinitude of peace'.

The first 'Caister Holiday Camp' was opened in 1906 by Fletcher Dodd in the grounds of his house on Ormesby Road. Known as the Socialist Camp this soon expanded to become the first holiday camp in England.

Small wooden chalets and tents formed the accommodation at the camp in the 1920s and 30s. The organisation was very much do-it-yourself and any entertainment was arranged by the campers themselves. The dining tent can be seen in the background. In 1924 a week's holiday cost 2 guineas (£2.10) inclusive of meals and transport to the station.

In 1933 the grounds of the Old Hall were developed into a camp site, wooden chalets providing the accommodation. This was soon followed by the Grasmere and Sycamore camps.

In the 1920s the number of holidaymakers steadily increased and Caister was firmly established as a holiday area. The beach was popular and tents became a common site in the summer months. In the background is the Manor Hotel.

The Manor House was built in 1793 and converted into an hotel in 1894. In the 1920s it was extended and had thirty-six bedrooms, billiard room, smoke room etc. The grounds covered thirteen acres with tennis courts and formal gardens overlooking the sea.

Coastal erosion throughout the 1930s destroyed, first, the gardens and then, in 1941, the house itself became a victim of the sea. The following year saw the destruction of the remainder of the house and today the Never Turn Back public house stands close to the site of the old hotel.

Caister railway station was opened in 1877. The M&GN line was closed in February 1959 and the station buildings were demolished early in the 1970s and houses, numbers 15 to 33 Manor Road, built on the site. The building to the right is the Methodist chapel.

STATION AND CAFE, CAISTER CAMP, CAISTER.   6741

In 1937 a railway halt was built at Caister Camp to enable the 'holiday camp expresses' to stop en route from London to Yarmouth. The halt buildings, seen here in the 1950s, are today used as a cafe. This was also the main camp access to the beach.

A delivery lorry outside the corn store of Arthur Hollis on the corner of Beach Road in the 1930s. The firm also had a large shop in Yarmouth Market Place. The shop is today a funeral parlour.

Charles Hunn butchers shop in the late 1920s in Yarmouth Road. The shop is still a butchers but is now Rackham's, .

Mrs Postle and her daughter outside their grocery and greengrocers shop in Beach Road in the 1930s. Today this is the Beach Road Chippy.

Mr and Mrs Vincent in their cart outside their general store on the corner of Beach Road, now the Co-op chemist. In the background is the large house in the High Street, demolished in the 1960s and known as the 'doctors house'.

The Kings Arms is the oldest public house in the village. Walter Julier was landlord from 1916 until 1935. Several forms of transport are lined up outside including a horse, a three-wheeled bicycle and a three-wheeled motor vehicle. The Kings Arms was rebuilt in 1935.

The Lord Nelson in Beach Road was built early in the nineteenth century and stood on the corner of Beach Road and Lacon Road. This Lacon's house was demolished in 1977 and houses were built on the site.

The Ship public house was built in 1815 and was the local for the beachmen and lifeboatmen. For nearly seventy years a member of the Haylett family was landlord and John Haylett was also lifeboat coxswain for several years.

The Green Gate and High Street in 1933.

The High Street in 1964 just before all the property on the left of the road was demolished to widen what was known locally as 'the narrows'. The old building on the corner was the wheelwrights shop and blacksmiths.

Church corner 1949. The bus queue on the left are waiting against the wall of the Old Hall. The volume of traffic in the 1940s did not warrant any traffic control system at this road junction as it does now.

A Sunday School outing prepares to leave the Yarmouth Road chapel in the 1930s in a varied selection of horse drawn vehicles. The chapel, in the background, closed in 1979 and was demolished the following year, a house now stands on the site.

Clay Road *c.* 1900. On the left is one of the many net chambers to be found in the village at that time where the 'beatsters' repaired and made nets for the Yarmouth herring fishing industry.

A group of 'beatsters'. These women worked in the net chambers in the village repairing fishing nets. This was a major source of female employment in Caister at the turn of the century.

Croquet was a popular pastime for some ladies and gentlemen in the last century. This group are playing on the front lawn of Caister House, High Street, in the 1880s when it was owned by the Morton family. This is now a doctors house and surgery.

Tan Lane in the 1930s. The shop on the left was the greengrocers of Helen Rudd, later Flaxman's fishing tackle. Further along, at number 9, was Haylett's tobacconist shop (see page 6) and at 13 George Tubby the butcher and later a fish shop.

William Allard's fruit and general store was in Tan Lane. Later converted into two smaller shops the house, Fern Lodge, was eventually restored to a private house.

Allen's garage, Yarmouth Road, in the 1930s. The business began with the shop on the right where George Allen made and sold bicycles and later expanded into the motor trade. William's garage stands on the site today.

The blacksmith's shop in the High Street *c.* 1900. Six generations of the Humphrey family were blacksmiths here until the business closed and the property was demolished in 1964 to widen the road.

Caister lifeboat crew 1903. The cowswain was James Haylett (centre row with the beard) and the gentleman on the left, behind the little girl, is Dr Case, for many years the village doctor.

The lifeboat *Covent Garden* in 1902. This was the third boat to carry the name and was stationed at Caister from 1899 until 1919. It was a 40 foot boat of the Norfolk and Suffolk design, rowed by twelve oars. In the background is the old mill which until 1906 stood in Mill Road.

The lifeboat *Nancy Lucy* was stationed at Caister from 1903 until 1929. Until 1929 there were two RNLI lifeboats stationed at the village. The RNLI station closed in 1969, the boats having saved 1,815 lives, a record for any station in the country.

The *Jose Neville* was Caister's first motor lifeboat and was stationed here from 1941 until 1964. Since 1973 the Caister lifeboat has been run as an independent service and still maintaining a full size lifeboat.

The Caister Rocket Company, March 1933. The Board of Trade Rocket Company was formed in the late nineteenth century and consisted of men who were not in the lifeboat service or fishermen. Among the people in this picture are Tom Jones, the village newsagent and Tom Humphrey, the blacksmith . The rocket apparatus was kept in the cart and the last occasion on which is was used was in 1919 at the wrecking of the *Moorside* (see opposite page). The company was disbanded in 1933.

The *Moorside*, a three-masted schooner, wrecked on Caister beach in 1919. The wreck was bought by the local blacksmith, Tom Humphrey, and broken up on the beach. The crew had been saved by the Rocket Company.

Houses on the warren to the north of the Manor House (see page 112). All twelve houses on the warren were destroyed by coastal erosion in 1941.

Helicopters were first seen in Caister in 1947 when an experimental mail service was run by the Post Office. Here the helicopter is taking off from a field on West Road.

A line of horse-drawn hearses, the funeral procession of those lost in the Caister lifeboat disaster of November 1901, seen here passing the Kings Arms on Sunday 17 November 1901.